A collection of poetry, prose, and quilt designs

Comforting Words

CARLA WRIGHT

Copyright © 2000, 2001, 2015, 2016, 2019 Carla Wright

All rights reserved. No part of this publication may be reproduced, distributed, or transmitted in any form or by any means, including photocopying, recording, or other electronic or mechanical methods, without the prior written permission of the publisher, except in the case of brief quotations embodied in critical reviews and certain other noncommercial uses permitted by copyright law. For permission requests, write to the publisher, addressed "Attention: Permissions Coordinator," at the address below.

Zeta Publishing, Inc
3850 SE 58th Ave
Ocala, FL 34480
www.zetapublishing.com

The views expressed in this work are solely those of the author and do not necessarily reflect the views of the publisher, and the publisher hereby disclaims any responsibility for them.

Ordering Information:
Quantity sales. Special discounts are available on quantity purchases by corporations, associations, and others. For details, contact the publisher at the address above.
Orders by U.S. trade bookstores and wholesalers. Please contact Zeta Publishing: Tel: (352) 694-2553; Fax: (352) 694-1791 or visit www.zetapublishing.com

First published by WestBow Press

Rev. Date: April 2019

ISBN: 978-1-947191-74-7 (sc)
ISBN: 978-1-947191-75-4 (e)

Library of Congress: 2018939036
Printed in the United States of America

This book is dedicated to
My daughter
Angela "Norie" Coleman

ACKNOWLEDGEMENTS

Many people deserve many thanks: First, Stanley Tipton whose support I cherished; then, to Renee' Anderson and Malisa Abrahams for early reviews, ideas and encouragement; and to my late parents (Harold and Eleanor Wright), siblings and their spouses (Phil, Mark and Erica, Jackie and Isaac, Marci, and Andrea and Todd), and best friend, Donna Willis — for recommending refinements, and always being there for me.

Foreword

For many years, I have written on scraps of paper here and there to keep before me, and God, my thoughts and feelings about life's joys and sorrows — sometimes ranting and raving, but always turning to God.

From those scraps came these poems and this book. It is about my life and God's place in it. Hopefully, readers will be encouraged to strengthen God's place in their lives.

I chose to pair these writings with quilt designs, as a tribute to quilters and the wonderful things they do with scraps. My sister, Jackie, recently gave me a refrigerator magnet that reads:

> "When life gives you scraps, make a quilt."

-The Author

POETRY AND PROSE

Precious Child	13
Norie	15
Go with God	17
It is Finished	19
Divorce Attire	21
Dinner Hour	23
Phone Call	25
Singles Retreat	27
<u>Romance</u>	29
Chosen	31
Where I Belong	33
Anatomy of a Godly Woman	35
Eleanor	37
Brianna	39
Tonisweet	41
Granny Crews	43
Jackie	45
Marci	47
Andrea	49
Keep Me	51

Quilt Designs

Baby Girl	14
Fun and Games	16
Centerpiece	18
Death and Life	20
Whispers of Love	22
Sharp as a Tack	24
Argyle	26
Sophistication	28
Fish and Flowers	30
Beauty Behind Bars	32
Sonshine	34
Coming of Age	36
Think Message	38
Hope for Tomorrow	40
The Sky is the Limit	42
Granny's Work	44
Medal of Honor	46
Follow Her	48
Perseverance	50
Unseen Power	52

Precious Child

We are in love
I have conceived
A heartbeat
A kick
No rest

Labor begins
Baby's distressed
They take her
She's here
Stand by

She cries so strong
You smile and touch
I answer
With tears
Of joy

God gives to us
A precious child
Our union
Has life
And breath

(For my daughter,
Angela "Norie" Coleman)

BABY GIRL

Inspired by the birth of my daughter,
the pastel colors and flowing ribbons
speak of a time when all was soft and sweet.
May her beauty and innocence
forever remain unmarred.

NORIE

Raven hair
        almond eyes
                cutest nose and chin

Rosy lips
        pretty legs
                freshest honey skin

Baby once
        lady now
                woman soon to be

Teach her well
        love her much
                sadly set her free

Fun and Games

Beach balls and sunbursts bring to mind
perfect summer days and non-stop fun.
There is no sweeter sound
than the joyous laughter of little girls at play.

Go with God

Just yesterday, you boarded a school bus
    for the first time
I took the day off to reflect on the milestone
I was concerned about who would protect you
    and how I could ever begin to let go
There was also some excitement
    over all that you would learn
    as you took your first ride into
    the real world
My mood was melancholy
    my baby was growing up

Today you're 18
I am reflecting on the mileage that brought us
    to this rest stop
    where you will now take the wheel
I have realized that protection can be stifling
    and that my letting go
    opens the door to your potential
    and gives responsibility its rightful place
There is some excitement
    over how you will use what you learn
    to become who it is you want to be
My mood is complex, undefined,
    and much less important than yours
    as you continue your journey
    in the direction you choose
    and at the pace you desire
My little girl is a young woman
Go with God

CENTERPIECE

Braided ribbons come together to form a
cross in the middle, a symbol of Christ-centeredness.
As our daughters become young women,
we pray they will be centered in the Lord.

It is Finished

Just before it was final,
I was so scared.
I stared at the phone, agonizing.
Call him — no, don't.
I suppressed the urge
And cried and cried.
The fear of being alone was not gone.

Inner turmoil gradually gave way
To fatigue and the dull ache
Of an ever-present, unanswered "why"

I don't understand what happened.
I still don't want to be alone.
I resent the loss of control
And the seemingly nonchalant
Infliction of pain by someone I cherished.

I have learned to trust in
And submit to God.
I cling to the new,
Vital relationship with Him
Grown out of the death of a marriage.

DEATH AND LIFE

Darkness and tombstones give way
to crosses and arrows
as dependence on God leads to
new possibilities after divorce. There is life
after the death of a marriage.

Divorce Attire

High-powered black suit?
    No, not today.
Besides, my high-heeled black shoes
    That make such a strong statement
    Are too tight, and they hurt my feet.
I'll be more comfortable enveloped
    In the lavender and violet ensemble
    My mother made for me.
It makes a statement
    That I alone can hear.

WHISPERS OF LOVE

Four hearts combine to hint at the magnitude
of the love that flowed from my mother's heart.
the ribbons are indicative of the special touches
apparent in all that she did.
A loving, godly mother
is a precious gift.

Dinner Hour

rapping a stack of papers on the table
to neaten them up
her demeanor screams efficiency
and officiousness
wonderful qualities in a corporate climber
but sadly misplaced
at the dinner hour
in a posh restaurant
on Sunday evening

do not dare suggest that she might
enjoy some company
the company is all she needs
and all she has time for
be careful not to disturb the well-ordered life of
one sitting alone
at the dinner hour
in a posh restaurant
on Sunday evening

to mask her loneliness she radiates confidence
(which is to her an impregnable force field)
she eats and works under the canopy of
feigned satisfaction
at the dinner hour
in a posh restaurant
on Sunday evening

a glance is noticed but not acknowledged
unable to become more approachable
and fearful of being approached
she calls for the check
at the dinner hour
in a posh restaurant
on Sunday evening

SHARP AS A TACK

Bow ties and flowers blend
almost imperceptibly in this design.
Femininity and professionalism
are not mutually exclusive notions.

Phone Call

Hearing from you is pleasantly unsettling.
Not hearing from you is sadly predictable.

Hearing from you makes me smile and hope.
It threatens to fill me with distraction
If not complete preoccupation.
Not hearing from you is less exciting;
It is, however, easier to accept and work around.

You said you'd call again.
I hope you do.
Until then,
The hope is tucked away
In a cozy corner of my subconscious mind.

I won't hold my breath,
But I'll gladly receive the call
As a pleasant surprise
If it ever comes.

Argyle

A traditionally male design
is combined with nontraditional colors
because they are not really all alike.
Do not judge all men
by the thoughtlessness of one.

Singles Retreat

I asked God to speak to me this morning
        in spite of things I may not like,
        understand, or agree with
I asked Him to let me know what He would have me do.
He gave me peace of mind, removed my guilt
        and said to me, "It will be all right."
I am warmed by the sun on my face
        and the Son in my heart.

The session on sex:
Key Points:
        God's standard has not changed.
        You have a right to ask God's help
        in order to comply with something He requires.

My thoughts:
The group seems to be comfortable
        with a cursory look at sex.
I need to go a little deeper to deal with
        the pressing realities
        surrounding the issue for me.
What should we do
        when we have followed all of the advice
        and asked for help, and we are still in trouble?
I guess what is needed is a change of heart.

There is no way for me to have peace
        over physical expression with a man
        as if we had made a full and complete
        commitment to each other
        if, in fact, we have not –
        in spite of strong attraction and affection.
I must express my feelings. I must please Him.
Those who cannot cooperate with me must be expelled

God help me.

SOPHISTICATION

Blocks indicating a straight path are contrasted with
blocks that seem to be going in circles –
much like we are with the things we try to justify.
God help us get back on the right track.

ROMANCE

If by chance
I find romance
Please let him be one of Yours

If Yours he is
I can be his
And worry I will no more

Tender glances
And smooth slow dances
Send us through love's secret door

If not for me
Then let me see
Before our hearts start to soar

I need to know
With me he'll go
To meet You when time's no more

Then our romance
Not by some chance
Will find peace on heaven's shore

FISH AND FLOWERS

Linking my husband's favorite thing (fish)
with my favorite thing (flowers),
two very different things are asked to work together
on the same project. Loving, romantic relationships
make the same request and much like this design
are both dark and bright.

Chosen

I am a woman
Chosen to be strong

Chosen to stand alone
High above the ache of loneliness

Chosen to flee lust
Disguised as longed-for love

Chosen to spin success
From frayed strands of mismatched yarn

Chosen to touch hearts
Scared to speak their piece

Chosen to confess weakness
When strength is needed most

Chosen to empty myself
For the joy of being filled

I am a woman
Chosen to be strong

BEAUTY BEHIND BARS

This design came after worshipping with a group of
women in a substance abuse recovery program.
the flowers are vibrant women coming together
to encourage each other in spite of the dark and heavy obstacles
through which their potential must break.

Where I Belong

Tattered and torn,
Feeling unloved and unlovable,
I find the energy to pierce the engulfing darkness
And lift my heart toward heaven.

Seated on a great throne
A large figure enshrouded in white
And radiating warm, bright light
Beckons me, "Come."
I raise my head, and His eyes full of fire
Meet mine full of tears.

I kneel at His feet, and my head bows
From the weight of my unworthiness.
I grab the hem of His garment,
And slowly pull myself up.
Clinging to His legs, I climb higher; and then
With all my might, I lift myself onto His lap.

Clutching His white robe,
I curl up and lay my head on His massive chest.
He folds His strong arms around me,
And I am comforted and warm.
My tears cease; my mind and heart stop racing.
I am at peace.

It is there, resting in His arms, I beg His pardon
For having doubted His love for me;
        And I renew my vow to love Him forever.

SONSHINE

Darkness dissipates the closer we get to the Son;
and the light of His truth draws, warms and soothes.
There is only one place that is always safe and warm –
in the Son.

Anatomy of a Godly Woman

She is all woman from her head to her toes
And a real woman knows
God's Word is a lamp unto her feet
And a light unto her path

She is all woman — pretty legs, caring arms
And a real woman's charms
Go beyond the movement of her hips
She walks in paths of righteousness and is oh,
So careful about whom she puts her arms around

She is all woman – sweetest mouth, keenest ears
And a real woman hears
Not what she wants to
But what is actually said in word and deed
She does not raise her voice to nag or brag, but
Lifts it to speak words of wisdom, comfort, and hope

She is all woman — classic nose, sparkling eyes
And a real woman tries
To see beyond the obvious
And smell trouble in time to flee it

She is all woman — open heart, open hands
And a real woman stands
For something and through everything
Giving, helping, lifting up the souls of others
And praises to God her one true King

She is all woman — bearing, feeding offspring
And a real woman brings
To the table this noble calling and so much more

She is all woman from her head to her toes
And a real woman knows
To hold her head high no matter what
As she taps her toes to the steady beat
Of a song in her heart

Coming of Age

This is a "sequel" to the Baby Girl design,
the same blocks are used with deeper, richer colors
and four of the blocks form a backdrop of a cross,
suggesting spiritual maturity.
Godly women are sure of their value and purpose.
They are strong in the Lord,
knowing that their help comes from Him.

Eleanor

She sang
      out of experience
           and from her heart

She sang
      and life was bearable
           and faith did grow

She sang
      and heaven came down
           and hope was real

She sang
      and darkness faded
           in love's bright light

She sang
      and shouting, weeping hearers
           surrendered

(In loving memory of my mom,
Eleanor Wright)

THINK MESSAGE

The four connected hearts that speak of my mother's love
appear again, this time at the heart of a cross.
The cross bears other hearts representing
those she connected with around the world
through her messages in song.
"Think Message" was her motto, and it helped her
bring hope and spiritual awakening to so many.
Her songs were heart-to-heart talks with God and any hearer.

Brianna

We rejoiced at your first breath and cry
    as your life began

And as your mother took care
    in preparing for that day
    it is our prayer that care
    and preparation taken now
    will lead to your rebirth in Jesus Christ

We lift you before God the Father today
    asking His blessing upon you
    and all the members of this village
    who promise to shower you
    with love and spiritual nurturing

We long for the day
    when the Holy Spirit will breathe on you
    and ignite new life in you

"A spring of joy inside that fills to overflowing"
    will move us to tears of sheer happiness
    on your re-birthday

(For my granddaughter on the occasion
of her Baby Blessing Service, with an
excerpt from "It's Raining Joy," a song by
Eleanor Wright, Brianna's late,
great grandmother)

Hope for Tomorrow

My first grandchild is a sweet little thing full of sugar
and spice. These blocks and colors say "Brianna" to me.
As she comes to know all that is her heritage,
may she use the best and rise above the rest.

TONISWEET

I call her Tonisweet because she is
And always has been
She is a real beauty
And a serious competitor
She has an unspoiled sense of fairness
And resists options that seem otherwise
She is building confidence
Asserting herself in a swiftly changing reality
Her tough and aggressive side
Can be surprisingly subordinate to
The spontaneity of a heartfelt response
Full of joy or compassion
I call her Tonisweet because she is
And always has been

THE SKY IS THE LIMIT

Toni has an incredibly sweet spirit.
She is discovering her many gifts,
and they will take her far.
The sky is the limit.

Granny Crews

A shawl and a rocking chair speak "grandma" to many

They speak "Granny Crews" to me

My mental picture of her was taken when I was 5

She was frail, living with aunt Eunice at De Soto Bass Courts

I later learned of the inconceivable quiet strength that sustained this kind, generous woman

Nora Bell Slaughter Crews was also a preacher's wife

And mother of my mom and her 13 siblings

She also took in an orphaned child making her mother to 15

She managed her home and did private duty work - all during the depression

Granny Crews was stylish and refined – humble, yet marvelous

She was truly grand

Granny's Work

Granny was an amazing multi-tasker,
who kept countless people
and complex matters
all together.

JACKIE

It's difficult to write about your hero
Because you're apt to use words they shrink from
Like role model, example, courageous
Heroes are not inclined to self-nominate
And tend to be keenly aware of reasons they would not refer to themselves as such
Heroes are not without flaw
Heroes have their flaws in check enough to rise above them and do the extraordinary
So I'll give my eldest sister, Jackie, a break
I won't call her my hero
I'll just say that courage is not something she has to muster
It's always there, just beneath the brilliance and depth of caring
Just know that if there is a standard to be upheld
Jackie is likely to emerge as the one who bares it
A powerful reminder of what is wise and just and right

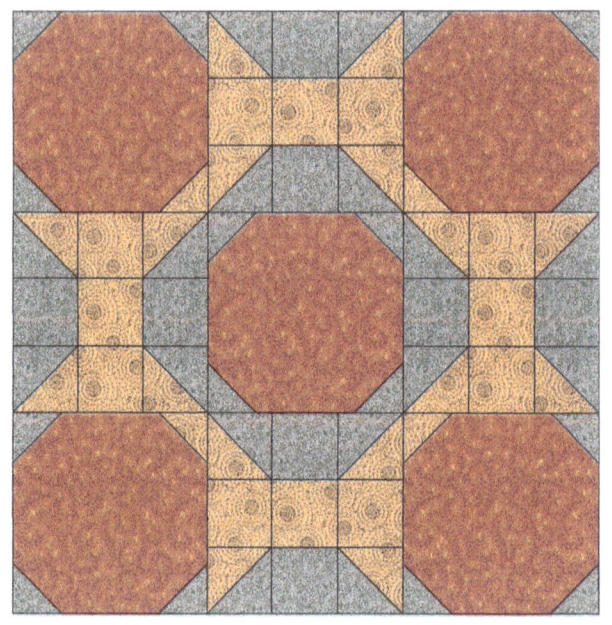

Medal of Honor

I believe Jackie deserves
a medal of honor.
She is not likely to agree,
but she might not mind
a quilted representation.

Marci

Three seconds after she enters a room

The unspoken consensus is that she should probably be in charge

As stylish as Mommy and as confident as Daddy, Marci has a uniquely elegant swagger

She can be very exacting and just as tender

She is a no-nonsense communicator and a baker whose mouth-watering pies speak "love"

Marci is a master healthcare advocate for her family,

Accepting no less than excellent medical care

And full patient compliance, which earned her the moniker: "Ninja Nurse"

Nothing is insurmountable to her, neither is anything a mystery

She has a quick and certain response to every question and without the aid of search engines

She is all of that and the sister closest to my age

The contentions of our youth have yielded

To the bonds of a loving friendship

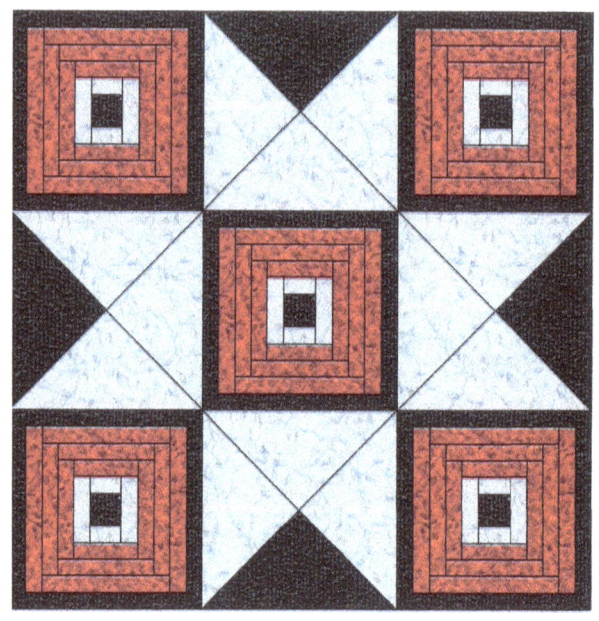

Follow Her

Marci's unwavering confidence
and keen eye for the best next step
make her worthy
to lead the way.

Andrea

Having a baby sister gives you an opportunity
To measure the impact of your influence
On the life of one who looks up to you
And to watch the emergence of a life
You helped water and nourish

One day, the effects of Sonlight
Accelerated Andrea's growth
And I found myself
Being watered and nourished
By her

I watched her negotiate difficult times
Taking one arduous step after another
She keeps going beyond the point
Where many would not
Now I look up to her

Perseverance

Her path has taken curious turns,
But still she presses on.
She knows that "a darker day
just calls for a little more of God's sunshine."
Her perseverance encourages me.

(Quote is from "The Blessing Is Already Mine," by Eleanor Wright)

Keep Me

When the wind grows
      from a gentle breeze
           to a stormy blast
                keep me

When the calm seas
      churn into an angry tempest
           keep me

When the sun hides
      behind racing dark
           hordes of clouds
                keep me

When the night sky
      forbids the stars
           in honor of pitch blackness
           keep me

But most of all
      when all is well
           keep me

UNSEEN POWER

Sails and windmills are evidence of the ability of an
unseen catalyst to evoke power and movement.
It takes an Unseen Power
to keep us moving in the right direction.

Comforting Words

Carla J. Wright has written her way through life's difficult and joyous milestones. Her love for poetry and quilts come together in this book to celebrate the beauty characteristic of both a colorful, comforting quilt and a poem that captures the essence of a heartfelt experience.

The daughter of the late Harold and Eleanor Wright, Carla has a daughter, Angela; a Son-in-law, Antonio; and three grandchildren – Brianna, Destoni, and Antonio, Jr.

Carla hopes this book will provide encouragement for women who value spiritual growth.

Carla J. Wright, *Owner*
Lydiaworks247@gmail.com

www.ingramcontent.com/pod-product-compliance
Lightning Source LLC
Chambersburg PA
CBHW061225070526
44584CB00029B/3994